MW01031389

I, the undersigned, MINISTER OF FOREIGN AFFAIRS of the Republic of Korea, hereby request all whom it may concern to allow MISS. MI-JIN KIM , a national of the Republic of Korea, proceeding to THE UNITED STATES OF AMERICA.

for the purpose of ADOPTION

to pass freely without let or hindrance, and to afford the aforementioned person such assistance and protection as may be necessary.

The validity of this certificate will expire on JANUARY 4, 1977 ,or upon the bearer's return to / arrival at / / / / / / / / / / / / / / .

Date. JANUARY 4, 1974

DESCRIPTION OF BEARER

Place of Birth: SEOUL, KOREA

Present Address: # 06-17, CHO-DONG, SEOUL.

Date of Birth: OCTOBER 12, 1971

Occupation: NONE

Height: 82 cm

Weight: 10 kg

Visible Peculiarities: NONE

Signature of bearer
PHOTO

a winner of the **2016 Open Book Contest**
selected by Carla Harryman

LITANY FOR THE LONG MOMENT

MARY-KIM ARNOLD

ISBN 978-0-9969229-3-7

Printed and bound in the United States
by Versa Press, Inc.

Cover design by Travis A. Sharp
Book design & composition by Aimee Harrison

Essay Press is a non-profit 501(c)(3)
organization dedicated to publishing
innovative, explorative, and culturally
relevant prose. www.essaypress.org

Distributed by Small Press Distribution
1341 Seventh Street
Berkeley, California 94710
spdbooks.org

10 9 8 7 6 5 4 3 2

Dear mr mrs Arnold

I received your nice letter
on 22nd Oct. I am glad that
mi jin's pictures. also I a
happy to see the child w

I also received the p

dress slip, vitamins, Doll
you sent for her, these the
when she goes to new hom
understand what for, but

Please don't send an
before she is reach to

Thank you every

Sincerely yours

On Soon Wha

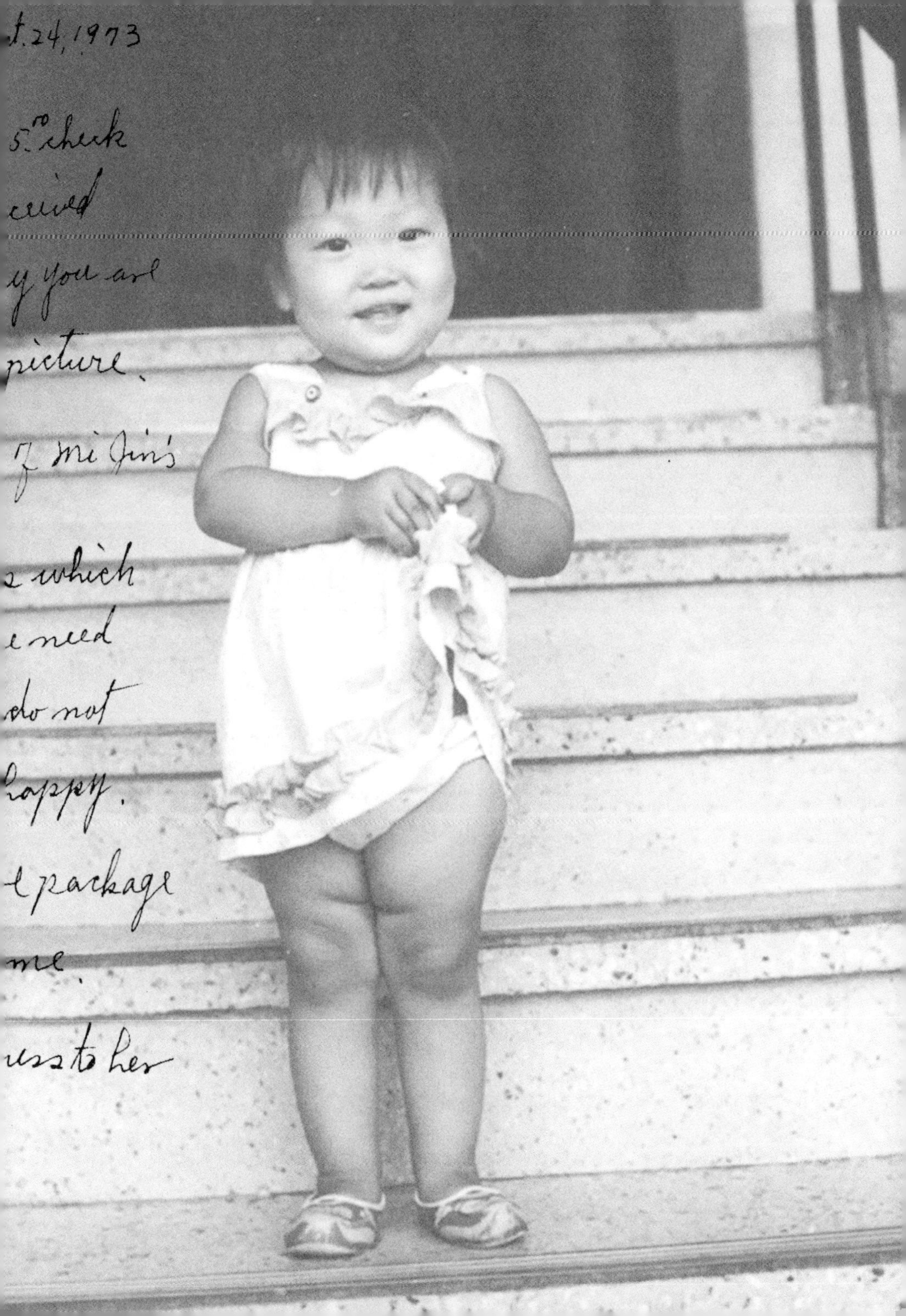

t. 24, 1973

5. check

ceived

y you are

picture.

of mi Jin's

s which

e need

do not

happy.

e package

me.

uss to her

I am sending you a three pa...
Please keep this pictures and t...
I do hope you will meet her s...
take care nicely. Please don't...

Thank You

CONTENTS

es of Mi Jin

all your family

he baby it.SS

up she is healty baby.

neirely yours

. Soon Whang (mre.)

INTRODUCTION

— CARLA HARRYMAN

A two-year-old Korean child disembarks from a plane in a new country. She is met by an American woman of Portuguese ancestry who states, "I am your mother." Years later, contemplating the notion that *language creates us*, she wonders, "Does language also destroy?" When the new mother states, "I am your mother," the writer asks, "Is the first mother destroyed?"

Litany for the Long Moment is an assemblage of concise and poetic responses to unanswerable questions grounded in memory's combining powers, and in the pronouncements and obscurities of the personal archive and public document. It is a work that seeks to retrieve impossible-to-access reality, which extends through and beyond the singular experiences of poverty and diaspora of the author's early Korean life and unforeseeable future trauma in the American world of the new mother. Arnold's deft employment of commonplace items, such as a graph of the Hangul alphabet or the Korean television program questionnaire, which she uses as a compositional prompt throughout the essay, guides the reader through a terrain of never-settled fact, difficult desire, and obscurity of persons and histories that animate her excursion into zones of personal and philosophical doubt.

One of the television show prompts asks, "When do you miss your mother or family the most?" Arnold responds to this dubious question with a salient one of her own, invoking the linguist Joshua Fishman's formulation that we can "only talk about what we can perceive and conceive." Thus, "our mind bares the imprint of embodied experience." Arnold links the normalizing assumption of the questionnaire, that one can pinpoint when one most misses one's mother, with Fishman's idea of shared, common experience in what one can perceive and conceive. But, Arnold wonders, if we can only talk about what we can perceive and conceive, what language struggles to emerge in "the small bodies of children making the six thousand-mile journey across the world"? This is a question, tragic and compelling, that connects personal biography to a collective biography sourced in the traces of experience that cannot be accounted for through any one idiom or theory.

Arnold's diasporic aesthetics are manifested both in her use of photographic images and captions, and in her haunting arrangements of composed and cited texts, which bring related but non-identical concepts and references into proximity. For instance, a citation of the Korean-American artist and writer Theresa Hak Kyung Cha resonates strongly with Fishman's idea of "imprint," but in a fashion that critiques rather than correlates with the linguist's assumptions. When Arnold cites Cha's artist statement, "the content of my work has been the realization of the imprint, the inscription etched from the experience of leaving," Arnold invokes an experience that requires new, rather than normalizing, conceptualizations of experience and subject matter within the context of emergent, diasporic art.

In the first pages of *Litany*, Arnold introduces her world of presences and absences in terse, poetic sentences that focus on the photographer

Francesca Woodman and Arnold's provisional identification with Woodman's *oeuvre*. Woodman is an artist who has attracted Arnold's attention partly because she lived in Providence, where Arnold has spent much of her life. Arnold's sense of literal proximity to the absent Woodman, who committed suicide at the age of twenty-two, cycles around another significant inquiry indicated by the "long moment" of the essay's title. Woodman's durational photographic practice, in which "the longer her shutter stays open, the blurrier and more transparent bodies will appear until at last, they disappear," powerfully resonates with the event of Arnold's sustained, reflective litany in which the haunting absence of her Korean mother and the death of her American mother opens to a consideration of trauma that is both specific to and extends beyond the singular life from a perspective that can only be illuminated through experiences of modern Korean history and the Korean-American's connection, however virtual, to this history.

This virtual feeling for existence that ties the Korean immigrant to the world that she has left is conceptualized in an essay by Seo-Young Chu, who identifies the feeling with what he calls "postmemory han."* Han is a form of grief that entwines personal and historical suffering within the Korean subject, while postmemory han involves the subject's second-hand experiences. This understanding of suffering, specific to the displaced subject, could contribute to a reader's understanding of Arnold's pursuit of impossible-to-apprehend relationships and events.

---

* For a comprehensive explanation of postmemory han see: Chu, Seo-Young. "Science Fiction and Postmemory Han in Contemporary Korean American Lit-erature." MELUS: Multi-Ethnic Literature of the United States, Volume 33, Issue 4 special issue, "Alien/Asian: Imagining the Racialized Future," ed. Stephen Hong Sohn (Winter, 2008), pp. 97–121.

Arnold's "writing into the rupture, the absence left there" is thus realized in a work situated in an ontological quandary that encourages a conjoining of the poetic and critical imaginations as well as a comic-tragic sensibility. Through both direct and indirect questioning of any document or given bit of evidence, Arnold both relies upon and interrogates theories of the photographic image, feminism, psychoanalysis, and language. Arnold has a particular ability to underscore the uncanny sense that any piece of evidence within the total assemblage of her text obstructs as much as it reveals: this goes for the essay itself. *Litany*, however, is not only a work of uncertainty, it is also one of generative linkages, "which intend no hard and fast correspondence" but instead provoke "reciprocal echoes, parallels, and allusion." The author's consideration of the works of Cha and Woodman, as well as the poetics of Myung Mi Kim, provides the context for the fabrication of a sagacious community of informant "sad girls" and an allusive aesthetic, one that exquisitely posits its own process of becoming. Arnold's *Litany for the Long Moment* is a compelling contribution to the essay form and to diasporic experimental literature.

PROLOGUE

In the photograph, Francesca Woodman is crouched in front of a wall. The plaster is chipped in places, and the floor is littered with debris. She is looking directly at the camera. Her polka dot dress hangs open. She covers her mouth with one hand and her breast with the other. Any intimacy the moment suggests seems staged.

I read about Woodman's short life before I had seen many of her photographs. About her artist parents, who imprinted her with a seriousness of purpose about the making of art. About her childhood spent between Denver and a village near Florence, Italy, where her parents had a second home.

She studied at the Rhode Island School of Design in Providence, where I have lived nearly my entire adult life. In the fall of 1979, she moved to New York, where in January 1981 she took her own life. She was twenty-one years old.

I mention the retrospective of her work to a friend who says with exasperation: "Oh, I've had enough of all the sad girls."

Those who knew her well will not call her sad. They will use the words exuberant, ambitious, and fragile to describe her. They will call her madcap. They will tell the story of how she once brought home live eels to watch them, the way their bodies moved. That she left raw meat to rot on her windowsill, to observe its properties over time. They will call her quirky, inventive. Intense. Irrepressible.

Not sad.

Was it the act of taking her own life that allows my friend to dismiss her as a "sad girl?"

And what an odd and arresting turn of phrase for suicide—"to take her own life."

I consider the term. I want it to mean something other than what it does.

Want it not to mean *ending* a life, but *claiming* it. Taking it in.

Of Woodman's work, the critic Elizabeth Gumport writes: "Woodman reveals the injuries that occur in the time it takes to produce a single picture: hair turns wispy, flesh fades and stretches into smoke. The longer her shutter stays open, the blurrier and more transparent bodies will appear until at last, they disappear."

I keep looking for her. In her photographs, her journals. In all the essays written about her.

I want to tell her: I see you. You are seen.

To her classmates, she once commented on being the subject of her own photographs: "I am as tired of looking at myself as you are of looking at me."

I think I understand this weariness, too.

Gumport refers to the "particularly long development process" that Woodman was experimenting with before her death. A single photograph could take hours to produce. "In the end," she suggests, "her camera captures not the girl but the long moment it looked at her."

My work, until now, in one sense
has been a series of metaphors for
the return, going back to a lost time
and space, always in the imaginary.
The content of my work has been
the realization of the imprint,
the inscription etched from
the experience of leaving.

—Theresa Hak Kyung Cha

Q1: WHO ARE YOU LOOKING FOR?

It is a reasonable question.

The longer I spend staring at the empty spaces on the questionnaire, the less straightforward it seems.

There is the mother, the father. Siblings. Aunts or uncles?

I am looking for anyone, everyone.

Some version of myself that I might recognize?

It's troubling that beginning should be so difficult.

Shouldn't I know, after all, what I want from all this looking?

My mother kept her few records of my adoption meticulously, and after she died my aunt gave me a single manila envelope with photographs, letters, official documents that I had not seen before. I shuffle through these periodically like the retired detective in a case long gone cold, as if one day I might discover something I had overlooked all these years. One small detail, a turn of phrase. And then I would know.

I. IDENTIFYING INFORMATION

Name: Mi Jin KIM
Sex: Female
Race: Korean
Date of Birth: October 12, 1971 (estimated)
Place of Birth: Unknown
Natural Parents: Both Unknown
Present address: Foster home in Seoul
Custodian: Social Welfare Society
Case #: 73-507-KIS

People like to speculate. I was told about the conditions of abject poverty in Korea after the war.

The lack of social services.

"Your mother could not keep you because she was so poor."

The social and cultural impossibilities of a woman raising a child alone.

"It's different for women in Korea."

My parents were both killed in a car accident.

This last possibility was the most seductive. It avoided the unanswerable question of *why*.

I will never know for certain what transpired in those first two years of my life. I only know that I am continually drawn back, tethered to the wispy, blurred possibilities of the mother I will never know, a language I do not speak, the life I will never have.

Q1: WHO ARE YOU LOOKING FOR?

At the Social Welfare Society of Korea, Shinhye Kang is the social worker assigned to my case.

I am #73-507-KIS.

Her signature informs me that she is a specialist in "Post-Adoption Services."

"I'm sorry," she writes after I submit all the necessary forms, "but the information you have is all we've got."

I go back to the manila envelope, look through the documents again.

"You've tried to contact us before," she reminds me.

A decade earlier, it seems, I had filled out the same forms.

"I'm sorry. We have nothing else to tell you."

Shinhye says that if I want, I can apply to appear on a Korean television show that reunites separated families. The show is called "I Miss that Person."

I find the awkwardness of the title rather charming, but it makes me think of missing as in targets. Like:

I am aiming at you but I keep missing.

I watch video clips online. The young smartly-dressed co-hosts speak earnestly on a garish set.

Shinhye sends me the application. "Please fill out this document, which is required from this TV program," she says. "Once I receive this document back from you, I will contact them."

There are four pages of unanswerable questions. Like:

"What is your opinion of Korea?"

And: "If you have had any difficulties that you faced in life, please explain in detail."

Q2. WRITE DOWN ANYTHING YOU KNOW ABOUT THE CIRCUMSTANCES LEADING TO YOUR ADOPTION OR ANY MEMORIES YOU HAVE. (EX: WHO FOUND YOU? WHERE WERE YOU FOUND? WHAT DO YOU REMEMBER?)

At two and a half years old, I was among the oldest children on the flight from Seoul to New York. I could speak in simple sentences. Could state my name and count to ten.

I was told that I was helpful. That I followed behind the flight attendants as they made their way up and down the aisles. I handed out toys, comforted babies when they cried.

Someone had made me a makeshift rattle with two plastic cups taped together and a few stirrers inside.

I was wearing a dress, a long-sleeved shirt. Someone had put a beret on my head.

But I do not remember any of this. It is only what I have been told.

Q6: HOW MANY TIMES HAVE YOU VISITED KOREA?
WHAT DID YOU DO THERE AND HOW DID YOU FEEL?

In 2000 I go back. The trip is for adult adoptees and supported by a South Korean government agency. They want to get to know us and for us to get to know the country, its language, history, and culture. There are more than two hundred thousand Korean adoptees living abroad.

In the year prior, the Korean government had passed the Overseas Koreans Act (OKA), officially recognizing ethnic Koreans who were living as permanent residents in other countries.

In their press release, adoptees are mentioned explicitly:

> Such individuals are unique and valuable assets to Korea While they are Korean in a biological sense, their American culture and lifestyles serve as a precious resource for the international development of Korea.

Had my mother still been living, I do not think I would have made the trip.

To her, it was a question of loyalty. Choose the mother who stayed over the mother who left.

She wanted it to be possible for me to start a new life, untethered to the past.

To her, it was a choice.

I didn't have the language then to say that those first two years were part of my life too.

My years. My life. I wanted to take it.

1122 Yonkers Ave. 4-H
Yonkers, New York 10704
January 26, 1972

Mrs. On Soon Whang
Orphans' Home of Korea
Central P.O. Box 83
Seoul, Korea

Dear Mrs. Whang:

Mr. and Mrs. Gottlieb gave us your name and told
us that you would be able to help us adopt a Korean
child.

We do not have any children and are anxious to
adopt a child.

Mrs. Gottlieb has told us such good things about
you and assured us that you would be able to help us.

We would like a little girl who is healthy and
intelligent and about three years old or younger. Mrs.
Gottlieb's little girl is beautiful.

Would you please send us any information you have.
We would appreciate any help you can give us.

I am sending $2.00 for postage because I know it
is expensive.

We will be looking forward to hearing from you.

Sincerely,

Mrs. Harry Arnold

II. SOURCES OF INFORMATION AND DATES

<u>June 25, 1973:</u>   ISS/AB asked this agency whether the child, who was at Orphans' Home of Korea, could be selected for overseas adoption placement.

<u>July 11, 1973:</u>   The Head of the Orphans' Home of Korea visited the agency with the child, and then the child was placed at the foster home of this agency.

<u>August 28, 1973:</u>   The child took medical test at Han Gang Sacred Heart Hospital.

<u>August 30, 1973:</u>   The worker of this agency interviewed foster mother, who came to our office with the child, and took information of the child's personality and habits.

DAY 1: KOREAN LANGUAGE I

We say our names aloud. We learn to count to ten.

Here in the classroom, we are children again, learning through rhyme and repetition.

We practice conversation:

What is your name?

My name is _____.

How do you do?

I am fine. And you?

Do you speak Korean?

No, I do not.

DAY 1: KOREAN LANGUAGE II

What day is today?

Today is my birthday.

What season do you like?

I like winter.

Which is your house?

That is my house.

I'll see you again.

I'll see you soon.

Yes, certainly.

Yes, I will.

Very well.

Koreans are proud of their alphabet. "Hangul is unique because we know who invented it," our instructor tells us.

Hangul is phonetic and its letters were designed to reference the parts of the body that are used to produce its sounds.

There are 19 consonants in Hangeul. You will learn the 14 basic consonants first. The basic consonants were modeled after the vocal organs; the mouth, lips, tongue, teeth, and throat.

ㄱ was modeled after the base of the tongue.
ㄴ was modeled after the tongue body.
ㅅ was modeled after the teeth.
ㅁ was modeled after the lips.
ㅇ was modeled after the glottis.

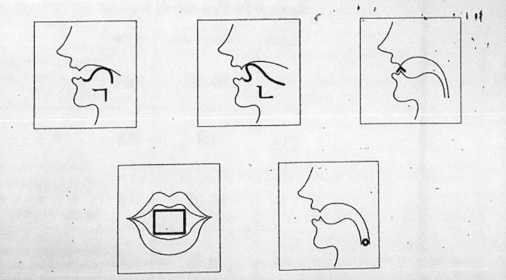

"It's a physical language," the instructor says. "When you speak it, you have to move your mouth. You have to move your whole body."

His lips are pursed to pronounce the *ooos* and *ohs* and he juts out his chin for emphasis. He bends his knees and bounces a little when he speaks.

"If you are doing it right," he says, "you'll feel the energy through your body."

"Do you feel it?"

I want to feel it.

Q8: WRITE ABOUT YOUR LIFE AFTER ADOPTION. ABOUT YOUR FAMILY, YOUR EDUCATION.

It wasn't until graduate school that I was introduced to the work of Korean American writer and artist Theresa Hak Kyung Cha. Cha is perhaps best known for her book *Dictée*, in which she weaves together biography, history, poetry, found text, and images to tell a story of alienation, dislocation, and the limits of language itself. It is also a story of contemporary Korea.

The speaker in *Dictée*, who has arrived "from a far," describes the physical experience of utterance:

> The entire lower lip would lift upwards then sink back to its original place. She would then gather both lips and protrude them in a pout taking in the breath that might utter some thing. . . . But the breath falls away. With a slight tilting of her head backwards, she would gather the strength in her shoulders and remain in this position. . . . From the back of her neck she releases her shoulders free.

Producing speech is not only physical, but there is discomfort, even pain when one wants to say something but cannot: "Inside is the pain of speech the pain to say. . . . It festers inside. The wound. . . . Must break."

I had been taught a few words in English and the night I arrived, I tried to speak. Tried out the words "hungry" and "toilet."

My first meal was bacon and fried eggs which I am told I ate with great delight. I am told in the latter case, my attempt to communicate my needs was less successful.

Speech, suggests Cha, is born in the body and must emerge from it:

> Now the weight begins from the uppermost back of her head, pressing downward. It stretches evenly, the entire skull expanding tightly all sides toward the front of her head. She gasps from its pressure, its contracting motion.

There is the sense that language itself must break out, emerge from its bodily container.

This from "Under Flag," by Korean American poet, Myung Mi Kim:

> No, 'th', 'th', put your tongue against the roof of your mouth, lean slightly against the back of the top teeth, then bring your bottom teeth up to barely touch your tongue and breathe out, and you should feel the tongue vibrating, 'th', 'th', look in the mirror, that's better

I am struck by how both passages foreground the apparatus of language, and the physical difficulty of making sounds that are unfamiliar.

For a time that night I was inconsolable. The exhaustion of travel, the confusion of landing in a foreign place. The embarrassment of soiled clothes.

Repeating a word loudly and with more urgency will only get you so far.

I am struck by the difficulty of saying one thing, but wanting to say something else.

19

Something for which you don't yet have language.

Something you may not yet know you want to say.

DAY 5: KOREAN LANGUAGE V

We learn that before 1446, Koreans did not have a writing system of their own. The educated elite wrote in hanja, classical Chinese characters, to record the meaning—but not the sound—of Korean speech. Chinese script, however, was ill-suited to the particularities of Korean grammar.

In 1443, King Sejong proclaimed that using hanja for the Korean language was "like trying to fit a square handle into a round hole."

He wanted a Korean alphabet that even common people could learn and use.

He gathered a team of scholars to develop this new alphabet and documented the process in the *Hunmin Jeongeum*: "The Proper Sounds for the Education of the People."

III. BACKGROUND INFORMATION

According to the referral information sent by the directress of the Orphans' Home of Korea, on June 20, 1973, the child was found abandoned at the Dongdoochun Babies' Home. And so, on June 26, 1973, the child was placed at Orphans' Home of Korea, trusted by Dongdoochun Babies' Home.

The child's name was given by the Orphans Home as Mi Jin KIM, which means: Mi—beautiful, Jin—true, KIM—a most common family name.

※ *Write your own name in Korean, Hangŭl.*

김	미	진	김	미	진	김	미	진	김	미
진	김	미	진	김	미	진	김	미	진	김
미	진	김	미	진	김	미	진	김	미	진
김	미	진	김	미	진	김	미	진	김	미
진	김	미	진	김	미	진	김	미	진	김
미	진	김	미	진	김	미	진	김	미	진
김	미	진	김	미	진	김	미	진	김	미
진	김	미	진	김	미	진	김	미	진	김
미	진	김	미	진	김	미	진	김	미	진
김	미	진	김	미	진	김	미	진	김	미
진	김	미	진	김	미	진	김	미	진	김
미	진	김	미	진	김	미	진	김	미	진
김	미	진	김	미	진	김	미	진	김	미
진	김	미	진	김	미	진	김	미	진	김
미	진	김	미	진	김	미	진	김	미	진
김	미	진	김	미	진	김	미	진	김	미

In emphasizing the intersections between a body of work whose subject is in fact the body, with a body of theory that renders the body problematic, I intend no hard and fast correspondences, no fixed equivalence. Rather, I am attempting a reading that provokes reciprocal echoes, parallels, and allusions between the work of theorists and the work of an individual artist whose relation to these theories, supposing it to have existed at all, is unknown.

— Abigail Solomon-Godeau

QI2: WHAT MOTIVATED YOU TO DO A FAMILY SEARCH AND WHEN DID YOU START?

When I look at the photographs taken at the Orphans' Home, I don't really see myself. I see a child, who appears familiar, in a landscape that does not. I see a moment, suspended in time.

I know something about the future that this child does not: I know the life that she has had is about to end.

"As a subject, I am always available," Woodman once said to her classmates. She used herself as the subject of most of her photographs.

As viewers, we know something about the future that she does not.

Critic Abigail Solomon-Godeau situates Woodman's work within feminist theory. Woodman herself never claimed a feminist orientation, nor did she use feminist language or explicitly define a political agenda. But her work consistently positions the female body as both an active producer of image and meaning, and as passive object, the receiver of gaze and of meaning—a thematic preoccupation that supports a feminist interpretation.

Woodman as subject was elusive. She is most often blurred or hidden, disappearing behind torn wallpaper, or barely visible in shadow.

As if to say I am here but I am not here.

To say you can look at me, but you cannot know.

Know, as in apprehend. Take in.

Woodman was twenty-one when she ended her own life, leaping from the roof of her apartment building in New York City. She was recognized, even at that young age, as having singular talent. Her photographs are haunting, enigmatic, resist easy classification. They stay with me. Her life story, the mystery at the center of it. The constant tension between seeing and being seen.

As a Korean child growing up in a white family, in a white neighborhood, what I was aware of most was being conspicuous. Rarely did I go unnoticed. Unquestioned.

But being visible is not the same as being seen.

Solomon-Godeau says that when Jacques Lacan said, "La femme elle n'existe pas," what he meant was that the category of woman is socially constructed and that subjectivity and meaning are all created in language.

The idea of woman can only be understood in relation to man and defined, therefore, by lack:

> And to the extent that the category woman is understood to be a wholly discursive production (and within patriarchy, a differential one; a being defined by her relationship to lack), conceptualization of the "real" woman is logically both unknowable and unspeakable.

I think about this in relation to Woodman's work, but also in relation to the category of orphan.

An orphan is understood to be without parents, defined by the relationship to lack.

Is orphan then similarly unknowable? Unspeakable?

The unspeakable orphan, defined by the lack of parents, can remain an orphan indefinitely, or become an "adoptee." The transformation can occur only if action is taken by others.

What actions can the adoptee take? What can the adoptee become?

VI. THE CHILD

<u>Physical appearance</u>: The child looks cute with round face, dark brown hair, ordinary back of head, thin eyebrows, black eyes, low nose, small mouth, round cheeks, olive-colored complexion. Her body has balance. She has 8 teeth on both sides.

What would happen if one
woman told the truth about her life?
The world would split open.

— Muriel Rukeyser

Q7: WHAT IS YOUR OPINION OF KOREA AND HOW DID YOU MAKE IT?

It is meant to be comforting, I think, but people like to tell me how I would not have been happy growing up in Korea. That women and girls are not valued, not considered equal.

That in Confucianism, traditionally, women have been expected to occupy the private sphere of domesticity while the public sphere is the province of men.

People like to tell me that I am better off here.

They use words like "lucky" and "blessing."

They shake their heads sadly for all the Korean children who are not me.

They mean well, I know.

But it does not feel lucky to be taken from one family and dropped into another.

You are looking at it the wrong way, people like to tell me. You're focusing on the wrong thing.

DAY 12: KOREAN LANGUAGE IX

When Hangul was first introduced, it was mostly women who used it.

We are not told this in class. I find this out on my own.

The aristocratic classes did not like this new, accessible language. It was threatening to their status.

Women wrote to record the experiences of domestic life. They passed down these *kyubang kasa*—literally, "lyrical verse of the inner room"—to their daughters.

Hangul became so popular among women it was referred to for a time—dismissively of course—as "women's script."

With it, women could preserve the details of their own lives, which historically had been hidden, and in their own voices, which historically had been silent.

Recognized as one of Korea's earliest women writers, Lady Hyegyong was born in 1735 and named Consort to Crown Prince Sado. She was taken from her home and moved into the royal court when she was nine years old.

There, isolated and alone, she wrote letters to her mother and father and they wrote back. She kept diaries of the complicated power struggles and political loyalties she witnessed.

Courtly life for Lady Hyegyong was tragic and traumatic. She saw the political executions of both her younger brother and her paternal uncle. She kept her memoirs to set the record straight—to defend their honor, and that of her father, who too was eventually imprisoned.

In the summer of 1762, Lady Hyegyong's husband, the Crown Prince Sado, was executed after years of madness, violent and erratic behavior, and relentless conflict with his father, King Yongjo. Court rules prohibited the shedding of royal blood, so the king ordered his son to be sealed into a rice chest, where he remained for eight days until he died.

In her final memoir, Lady Hyegyong recounts the history of this incident, addressing it directly in all its harrowing detail.

"Writing a memoir was a very unusual activity for a woman at that time, and Lady Hyegyong had to surmount formidable cultural obstacles to do so," writes JaHyun Kim Haboush in her introduction to *The Memoirs of Lady Hyegyong*. "First, she had to overcome an inhibition against self-narration."

She had to claim her own life.

This was not easy for her to do. Lady Hyegyong wrote:

> Compelled by these considerations, I forced myself to write. Many
> things were hard to speak of; some were just too painful to write
> about—and these amounted to quite a few in number—and I
> have left them out.

Q12: WHAT MOTIVATED YOU TO DO A FAMILY SEARCH AND WHEN DID YOU START?

In placing herself before the camera, Woodman attempted to collapse the distinction between subject and object.

It is her body in the frame for our gaze and yet our gaze is so often thwarted, interrupted, resisted.

In one photograph, an image of the woman holding the image of herself, and represented as if in an endless series of reproductions.

In another, she has wrapped her naked body in clear plastic. White rags on empty bookshelves behind her. The plaster walls crumbling. Her form barely visible through the plastic.

Poet and critic Ariana Reines points out the "fact that [Woodman] appears in her own photographs has caused many to mistake them for self-portraits which they are not."

Reines asserts that Woodman resisted the "merely documentary aspect" of photography to offer a kind of truth beyond simple disclosure.

To attempt to express this kind of truth—beyond the mere facts of disclosure, beyond the official documentation, the state records, the case files—

To leave some record of a life that resists reduction, simplification, erasure.

Q13: WHEN DO YOU MISS YOUR MOTHER OR FAMILY THE MOST?

In a book about Korean lineage records, I came across a sketch of a traditional Korean "Big House" and courtyard nestled at the base of mountains and surrounded by a low stone wall. Inside the gate, the open courtyard.

For years I dreamed this courtyard. Dreamed sleeping on its tightly-packed earthen floor, a flat stone beneath my head.

In the dream, I could hear my mother calling me just beyond the courtyard walls. But my body was heavy, like a great weight held me to the ground and I could not move.

In the dream, she called out to me for a long time.

Korea lacked charm or natural beauty
and was neither quaint nor rustic. It should
have been the last place on earth where
anyone would want to fight a war.

— Donald Knox

Q7: WHAT IS YOUR OPINION OF KOREA AND HOW DID YOU MAKE IT?

A man walks up to me in my high school gymnasium and by way of introduction says, "I know your people hate my people, so we could never be friends."

I learn later that his people are Japanese. And that he is referring to the occupation.

The 1876 Treaty of Ganghwa between Japan and the Joseon Dynasty opened the Korean peninsula to foreign trade. Known for centuries as the "Hermit Kingdom," Korea had long maintained a policy of isolation. This treaty became the first formal step toward what became the Japanese occupation.

During the thirty-five years of Japanese rule, Koreans were forced to adopt Japanese cultural and religious practices. For more than a decade, the Korean language—of which Koreans were so proud—was banned in schools, businesses, and public places under penalty of death. Koreans were forced to adopt Japanese names.

Cha likens this enforced renunciation of language to a kind of exile: "The national song forbidden to be sung. Birth less. And orphan. They take from you your tongue . . . "

The man and I dated on and off for a time. My mother did not like him. I did not meet his people.

Q13: WHEN DO YOU MISS YOUR MOTHER OR FAMILY THE MOST?

American linguist Joshua Fishman describes three distinct cultural functions of language: to express its overtones, concerns, artifacts, values, and interests; to stand for the culture and sum it up (the economy, religion, philosophy); and to hold the soul and spirit of a people, allowing people to recognize that they belong together, and compelling them to preserve their own continuity.

Infants learn language with their bodies. The more opportunities they have to move around and to interact with their world physically—by holding or shaking an object, for example—the better their ability to acquire the words to describe their environment.

"We can only talk about what we can perceive and conceive, and the things that we can perceive and conceive derive from embodied experience. This means that our mind bears the imprint of embodied experience."

I think of the small bodies of children making the six-thousand-mile journey across the world. Leaving one place for another, going back in time. What words have formed within them, what language struggling to emerge?

Q13: WHEN DO YOU MISS YOUR MOTHER OR FAMILY THE MOST?

Consider the degrees of your longing. Rank it:

    1—I miss my mother not at all
    10—I miss my mother most

and so on.

Missing is a dull constant ache buried deep in the body or—

Missing is sharp and hot. It sears.

When do I miss my mother? To miss is to notice the loss or absence of—

To miss her, wouldn't I need to remember her?

I feel loss. I feel absence.

I will name this absence mother.

DAY 4: KOREAN FOLK MUSEUM AND GAME

The Korean Folk Village is not a village, but the re-creation of a village. An open-air living museum. We wander the exhibits—models of traditional homes, mills, and shops.

Roving bands of actors and performers dance in costume. A traditional wedding parade marches through.

We do what we are expected to do: take photographs in front of the kimchi pots, buy postcards and fans to take home.

I want to be charmed by the tightrope walkers, the villagers in traditional dress. But I find the spectacle alienating.

Someone asks me if I feel anything, if being here helps me to remember anything at all. He means well, but I don't have words for what I feel, and so I shrug and wander away.

I feel complicit in a performance of Korean-ness.

Sometimes people think I should meet the Koreans they know.

A colleague takes me to a small photo processing shop a twenty-minute drive away. The owner is a Korean woman in her fifties. She speaks in halting English.

She tells about when she first came here, in her twenties. That she didn't know anyone, found work in a bar. The owner had been to Korea, said he knew how hard Koreans worked. That they were good, hard-working people.

"He told me he loved Koreans," this woman says.

But then he tried to take her home one night and she refused. He told her she was worthless and that she should go back to where she came from.

"He said I should be grateful for everything he did for me." She tells me this as we sit on stools in the cramped office behind her shop.

At the time of her death, Cha left fragments of a film she had been work-ing on called *White Dust from Mongolia*. It is a film about returning to Korea, after many years away.

She had emigrated with her family as a child, spent most of her life on the west coast, studying art and film. She had just recently married and moved to New York.

In 1982, on a night in early winter, Cha was murdered by a stranger.

She was raped and strangled. Her body was left in a parking lot. She was found with one boot on, the other several feet away. It was cold, and a light snow had been falling.

Always to insert her own body onto
the field of the problem, to
use it, understand it, as the ground
of whatever sense the image might
make, is the pattern that emerges
throughout the problem sets that
Woodman undertook.

— Rosalind Krauss

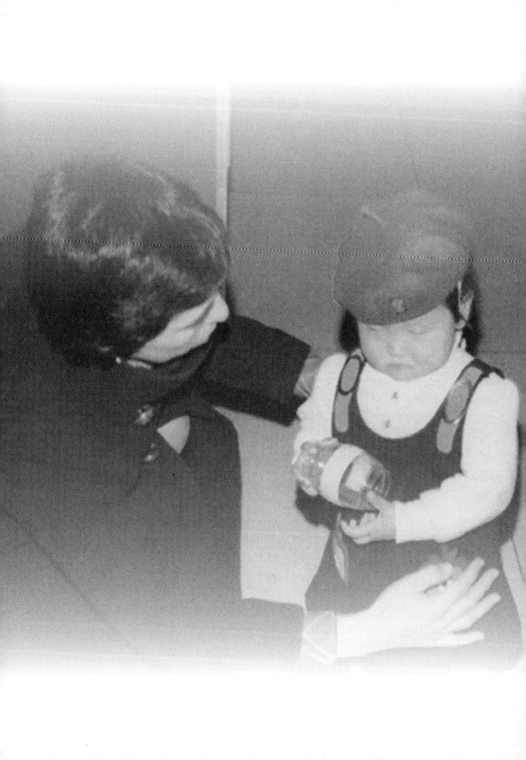

Q11: WHEN DID YOU KNOW YOU WERE ADOPTED AND HOW DID YOU FEEL ABOUT IT?

"Does it read as a book, one wonders?" Woodman writes this in her notebook about what she might leave behind. Did she think of this as she was composing her own work?

I wonder at times whether I am living my life or performing it.

Ariana Reines says Woodman is a "problem" because she is a "seducer" and "we love to be seduced."

For the camera? For the page?

Women are always a problem in desire and in language.

A child is a problem when there is nowhere for her to go.

Language is a problem because when I say "my mother," it can mean many things all at once.

Q12: WHAT MOTIVATED YOU TO DO A FAMILY SEARCH AND WHEN DID YOU START?

Among the documents my mother kept are: several copies of a three-page "social study" of which I am the subject; a record of medical examinations; letters from the director of the orphanage where I lived for some time; and a few photographs of me: as a child in Korea, as I arrived in New York.

Roland Barthes claims that every photograph contains its future death and is therefore catastrophic.

The death I see in the photograph of me at JFK is that of the child I was before. As if the flight itself erased one life and put in its place another.

Susan Sontag says that photographs provide "imaginary possession of a past that is unreal." It is both the possession that is imaginary and the past.

Although they offer evidence of experience, "taking photographs is also a way of refusing it—by limiting experience to the search for the photogenic, by converting experience into an image, a souvenir."

Souvenir, from the French, for the act of remembering.

But the photograph is also a kind of evidence: "to attest that what I see has indeed existed."

Barthes goes on to say, "The photograph does not necessarily say *what is no longer*, but only and for certain *what has been*."

The life is there, encased in its own death. Its own catastrophe.

DAY 8: VISIT ELEMENTARY SCHOOLS

We spend a day surrounded by Korean children: first, at an elementary school in the countryside. The students are bright-faced and loud. They are eager to have their photographs taken and they cluster and pose for us.

It is hard not to imagine what might have been. Other possible lives. Hard not to want to claim something these children have never had to doubt.

It is not envy. Or at least not envy entirely. Curiosity?

Who might I have been? And does something of that possible self—those possible selves—still reside within me?

Later we attend a Tae Kwon Do demonstration. Uniformed children in straight lines, making practiced movements on command.

We are invited to join them. To learn simple motions. The auditorium is large but airless.

I hold one pose and then another. I find it difficult to breathe.

When I collapse, it is from the heat, the intense humidity to which my body has not yet acclimated.

But it is hard not to think of it, too, as a small act of resistance. This is not me. This is not my life. I can adopt its postures, mimic its gestures, but I will not for one moment forget that none of this is mine.

DAY 7: RECREATION

On the trip, there is an afternoon set aside to tour the orphanages and to help us search for our families.

I tell myself I am not ready. I tell myself that there is time.

I watch from the dorm room window as the bus pulls away.

QI: WHO ARE YOU LOOKING FOR?

In the social study, there is mention of a foster family. A woman and her grown son.

I write again to Shinhye, ask her for a name.

She tells me the information is useless, untraceable. Post districts and phone number systems have changed. It's been so long.

I ask for what she has, anyway.

She writes:

"Her name was LEE Songhee and she was 45 years old at that time."

"She was living in Hongeun-dong, Seodaemungu."

"Her phone number was 352-1733."

Before she signs off, Shinhye says: "I hope this answers your questions."

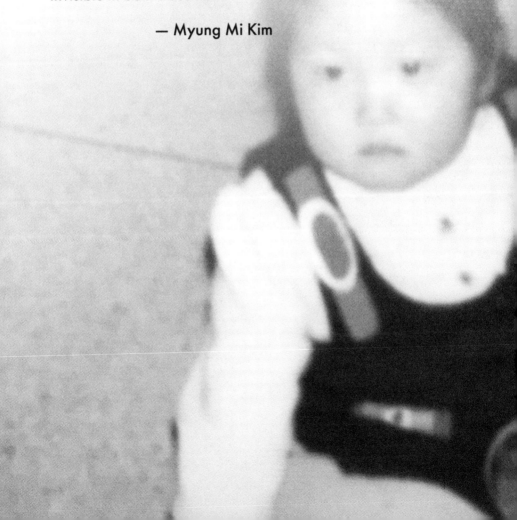

If Korean history is missing from
the master narratives of the
West and women are absent
from recorded Korean history,
the Korean American woman is
invisible in both discourses.

— Myung Mi Kim

Q9: IF YOU HAD ANY DIFFICULTIES THAT YOU FACED IN LIFE, PLEASE EXPLAIN IN DETAIL.

> "it dawns on me   just the other day that
> i have been back   back for months
> that i have lived here   since then
> it starts without me
> it started without me"

Cha wrote about returning in 1980 to a country she did not recognize. She found a modern-day Korea characterized by political turmoil and violence. Protests against dictator Park Chung Hee were being brutally suppressed with bloody military action. This was not the homeland she remembered.

Q10: HOW DID YOU OVERCOME IT?

I remember a dusty courtyard. Or the dream of it.

I remember feeding dried corn to wild turkeys as they strut along a chain link fence.

I remember the tender flesh of persimmon so sweet and so ripe.

On the trip, a man tells the story of how he watched his mother leave in a car one morning. He was sitting in the front yard of a neighbor's house. He did not know it would be the last time he saw her.

Q1: WHO ARE YOU LOOKING FOR?

Songhee Lee. Formerly of Hongeun-dong, Seodaemungu. Her last known phone number was 352-1733.

I find one Songhee Lee who is a dancer in New York. Another, a filmmaker although I cannot tell exactly where. I find several very young Songhees. My Songhee would be ninety years old.

QI: WHO ARE YOU LOOKING FOR?

Once we went back. I always forget. When I was four years old, my mother took me to see the child who would later become my sister.

She had been told there were people who should not know I was back in the country. That they might try to interfere. "It will be too confusing," she was told.

My mother wore a wide-brimmed hat and kept her head down. She hurried me through public places.

Q. I: WHO ARE YOU LOOKING FOR?

Songhee Lee had an adult son.

I dream he meets me in a hotel lobby while he is traveling for work. He brings me a box of papers that belonged to his mother.

He tells me he has come such a long way to meet me. He tells me he wants me to be at peace. That in the box I will find out everything I want to know.

I take the box home and sit cross-legged on the bed with it. But even as I reach out to open it, I know that it is empty.

Q1: WHO ARE YOU LOOKING FOR?

There is one name I have had from the beginning. From the letterhead of the Orphans' Home, handwritten on greeting cards and letters my mother saved.

On Soon Whang placed dozens of children overseas, arranging for their transport and even, on occasion, financing it. She had a college degree, at a time when few women were educated. She funded the Orphans' Home with her own money. She had family ties to the highest levels of government.

"I was glad to know that you would like to adopt a Korean girl," she wrote to my mother in 1972. "We have 44 girls (aged 7–14 years old) in our home now. But I will try to find you a younger girl if that is what you have wanted."

One year later, she wrote, "I am happy to tell you that your child is fine and in good health under the special care of the Social Welfare Society. Thank you for your kind letter and for enclosing your check."

DAY 11: VISIT DMZ

The Korean Demilitarized Zone was established at the end of the Korean War. It's is a strip of land that divides the Korean peninsula roughly in half. About 160 miles long and 2.5 miles wide, it is, despite its name, the most heavily militarized border in the world.

Our tour bus idles at the Bridge of No Return. At the end of the war, prisoners were given the choice either to remain in the country of their captivity or to cross over to their homeland, knowing it was a choice they could make only once.

The site itself is unremarkable—weeds sprouting up through cracked concrete, a crooked sign, rusted and faded.

Before we enter the Joint Security Area, we are required to sign a statement, agreeing to comply with the instructions of the United Nations Command.

We are told we must not point, make gestures, or expressions which could be used by the North Koreans as propaganda against the United Nations.

As our bus is leaving the area, it is flagged down and boarded by two uniformed men. One walks down the aisle and takes the camera from one of the women. If he says much, I do not recall. If she protests, I don't remember that either. He flips open the back, pulls out the film, tucks it into his pocket. He hands the camera back to her. I remember all this happening in silence.

After they leave, the doors of the bus hang open for a while, letting in the humid, stifling air.

Q10: HOW DID YOU OVERCOME IT?

People like to tell me that to give up a child must require a certain kind of optimism. A belief that the pain of relinquishing the child in the present moment can be borne in service to the future—a better life for the child. That for the promise of some future reunion, the separation can be endured.

I don't know whether I would characterize relinquishment and adoption this way. I suppose this interpretation contains an appealing notion of self-sacrifice. The romantic idea that a mother's love can transcend time and distance. That reunion can undo the past.

I don't mean to seem ungrateful.

The idea that separation must be endured is familiar to a nation that has been divided for most of recent memory. To the families who believed their dislocation might be temporary when the border line was drawn across the 38th parallel.

Theresa Cha, on returning to a nation, still divided:

> Here at my return in eighteen years, the war is not ended. We
> fight the same war. We are inside the same struggle seeking the

same destination. We are severed in Two by an abstract enemy an invisible enemy under the title of liberators who have conveniently named the severance Civil War. Cold War. Stalemate.

Q10: HOW DID YOU OVERCOME IT?

In the reunion fantasy, everyone waits.

I remain tethered to abstractions—mother, motherland, mother tongue.

This holding pattern—

any day, some news will come from a far and I will be called home.

Waiting is a kind of exile.

I don't mean to seem ungrateful.

The DNA tests. The search registries. The message boards.

The letters to social workers. The television talk shows.

The questionnaires.

Days, months, and years of waiting.

To wait is to remain orphaned, indefinitely—

QI: WHO ARE YOU LOOKING FOR?

On Soon Whang sends letters to my mother in the months before my arrival.

She writes, "I received the package of Mi Jin's dress, slip, vitamins, doll, socks, which you sent for her, these things she needs when she goes to her new home. She does not understand what for, but she is happy."

And later, "Your dear daughter is healthy and playing with the doll you sent her. She is so happy these days."

In the last letter before my arrival, she writes, "I went to visit Mi Jin the other day. She acted like I was a stranger. I thought, how easily the child forgets."

Q9: IF YOU HAD ANY DIFFICULTIES THAT YOU FACED IN LIFE, PLEASE EXPLAIN IN DETAIL.

My mother is dying and I have left school to be at home. Through the summer and into the fall. I skulk around the house while she sleeps. I take walks.

I find a latch hook kit in a closet and so I spend an afternoon folding lengths of yarn and hooking them through a plastic mesh mat. It's a Dalmation puppy on a red background. It's horrible, but I like keeping my hands busy.

I'm bored and lonely and my college friends are backpacking across Europe or taking internships in DC. One friend stops through town on her way to New York City and brings me a carton of French cigarettes, so I smoke in the backyard when no one else is around. When the hospice nurse starts coming every day, I stop.

I show my mother the Dalmation and she makes approving noises. She's on pain medication and groggy. She says, "Maybe you could make a flower right here and points at the dog's head." I say, "Yes, that's a good idea, I will."

At night, I dream of her young. She is wearing a yellow dress and her hair is long. I dream sunlight behind her, illuminating her as she walks.

My father did odd jobs—deli clerk, late-night security guard at a nearby hospital. Scribbled song lyrics and chord notations on scraps of paper while he worked. He taught himself magic tricks and showed them to me when we were in the house alone. "Your mother thinks this is stupid," he would say, "so don't tell her."

He left when I was ten. My mother took me to the shore. We stayed on the second floor of a double-decker house that we rented a week at a time. There was a wide wooden porch where we sat in the late afternoons until a family with three boys moved in downstairs.

They spotted me as they unloaded their car, pointing fingers and calling out, "Attack! It's Pearl Harbor!"

They ran in circles on the sidewalk, making shooting sounds with their mouths.

I did not know anything about Pearl Harbor then, and I suspect that what they knew was limited too.

Later, when I learned about the Japanese, I wanted to go back and tell them: "Korean. Not Japanese. There is a difference."

But back then, it did not matter.

On the playground, I was only ever Chinese or Japanese.

"Korea, the country. It's where I was born. Korean."

"No. You're either Chinese or Japanese. Which?"

The boys downstairs did not stay long. After a few days, I watched from the porch as they dragged their things from the house to their car, idling at the sidewalk. Then the house was quiet again, the battle won or surrendered: it was not quite clear which.

As a child, I was a dancer. For several years, I had an agent who sent me on auditions for commercials. That summer, when I was 10, we made trips back into the city from the beach house.

Auditions were long, unglamorous affairs and we were often kept waiting for hours in leotards and tights, our hair in topknots. Finally, we'd be assembled into lines and ushered into a room where we would be asked to walk back and forth in front of a wall of mirrors while someone took notes. Then someone else would demonstrate a dance combination and we'd all try to reproduce it.

Once I was the last girl left in the room after everyone else had been dismissed. I was asked to let my hair down. Then hold it up again. Can you make a worried face? Can you look confused? Can you hold your hands to your mouth like you have seen something you wish you could forget?

They took photographs of these poses, so that later they could remember. The kind that developed instantly. The click of the camera, and then the low buzz as the photo slid out—the image blurred and unknowable until at last, recognizable patterns emerged from the field of white—a face, a hand, a mouth in focus inside the frame.

While my mother and I stayed at the beach house, my father was packing the last of his things into cardboard boxes and trash bags.

He left behind a few plastic hangers in the front hallway closet. A neat pile of matchbooks from neighborhood bars and restaurants.

And later, after he had been gone for weeks, on the floor of his closet, I found a photograph he had perhaps not intended to leave.

I am sitting on his lap. His head is turned away, and I am facing the camera. I am wearing a blue dress, leaning back against his chest.

Peggy Phelan: "Our encounter with the photograph always occurs after the event recorded within it. The belatedness of photography reminds us of our tendency to arrive too late and perhaps especially to arrive too late to appreciate the unique drama of our own mortality."

QI1: WHEN DID YOU KNOW YOU WERE ADOPTED AND HOW DID YOU FEEL ABOUT IT?

Among my mother's documents, I find a small yellowed booklet that includes basic Korean vocabulary. Korean children learn English very quickly, the reader is assured.

There is some research that bears this out. Adopted children are highly motivated to learn the language of their new families and tend to do so quickly. They also tend—since very rarely is the native language maintained by the adoptive family—to lose their first language.

Q10: HOW DID YOU OVERCOME IT?

Literary theorist Stanley Fish says that "sentences promise nothing less than lessons and practice in the organization of the world." Language creates us, he says.

If language creates us, can language also destroy?

On a night in late spring, with a dusting of late snow on the ground, an American woman, daughter of Portuguese immigrants, says to the Korean child disembarking from a twenty-hour flight: "I am your mother."

"Language is not a handmaiden to perception; it *is* perception," says Fish. "It gives shape to what would otherwise be inert and dead. The shaping power of language cannot be avoided."

A new mother takes shape. Is the first mother destroyed?

English	Korean
Where is the pain ?	Eoh-di-ga A-poo-ni ?
	머리가 아프니 ?
Are you very ill ?	Man-yi A-poo-ni ?
	많이 아프니 ?
Are you ill a little ?	Zo-kum A-poo-ni ?
	조금 아프니
Take the medicine !	Yak-meok-za.
	약 먹자.
It is bitter !	Ssui-da.
	쓰다.
Is it bitter ?	Ssui-ni ?
	쓰니 ?
Is the medicine bitter ?	Yak-yi Ssui-ni ?
	약이 쓰니 ?
It is not bitter.	Ssui-zi An-ta.
	쓰지 않다

Q9: IF YOU HAD ANY DIFFICULTIES THAT YOU FACED IN LIFE, PLEASE EXPLAIN IN DETAIL.

At some point in my teens, everything changed. This was before she got sick.

We fought all the time. I was too independent or not independent enough. I stayed out late and drank with boys.

I loved someone she did not approve of.

"You will end up just like your mother," she would say.

Finally, I leave for Providence. I don't intend to return.

Q10: HOW DID YOU OVERCOME IT?

In the final days, we think we know what it means that she is dying.

When she coughs it makes a hollow sound, like a sudden breeze through reeds.

She tells me what she wants me to save when she is gone. A box of photographs on the floor of her closet.

Two wool dresses, still with their tags. A hat she bought one spring but never wore.

I watch her sleep. Her skin so pale, her body so light it seems she must be floating, the tangle of white sheets her only tether.

Death does not only cast its shadow over the images that remain, but suffuses them with a strange, spectral light.

If living is a slow erasure of the self, does dying fix it in place?

Barthes, on dying: "The photograph mechanically repeats what could never be repeated existentially."

Either you will
go through this door
or you will not go through.

If you go through
there is always the risk
of remembering your name.

— Adrienne Rich,
from "Prospective
Immigrants Please Note"

DAY 5: KOREAN LANGUAGE IV

Our instructor tells us that Korean sentences are ordered as either:

    subject + verb, or
    subject + object + verb.

There is no verb inflection for tense or number. There are no articles. Relative pronouns are not used and there is no gender agreement with pronouns. Passives are not commonly used. Many verbs are not subject to being passivized.

He makes up, on the spot, a silly anecdote to illustrate the difference between Korean and English syntax.

Your friend calls you on the phone, he says, and the connection is not good. You want to tell your friend to bring you an apple. In English, you would say:

"I want an apple."

But the phone cuts out before you finish the sentence. So all your friend hears is "I want," and she would never know what it was you wanted.

In Korean, you would say:

"I apple want."

Your friend would hear the important words—you and apple. Your friend would know something about you and about the apple. Or, in Korean, you could just say "apple," and assume that your friend knows it's about you and could probably conclude that you want an apple. And then she would bring it to you.

We all laugh. But I want more.

I want to know: Is the fact that a relationship exists between the subject and the object of the sentence more important than the nature of that relationship? Or more important than the action that transpires between them?

QI2: WHAT MOTIVATED YOU TO DO A FAMILY SEARCH AND WHEN DID YOU START?

I want to believe I carry Korea in me, in my blood and bones.

That my body remembers something of my mother, my father, my first home.

That Korean-ness lies dormant, waiting.

That maybe language is one way back.

If I can learn its grammar and alphabet

hold its vocabulary in my mouth

then perhaps I can know something of history—my history.

If I can speak it, then maybe I can know its topography—

the rugged mountains that run down the peninsula like a broken spine,

wild river that bisects its cities.

If I can name its flora and fauna, its national flower,

if I can sing its national anthem,

if I can learn the right words for mother, for longing, for love,

then maybe I can recover some lost thing.

I fear this is asking too much of syntax.

<u>Worker's Comment:</u> She lives well with foster family, especially foster mother. As she has the habit of sucking empty milk bottle, she sometimes takes the breast of foster mother, which has not milk now.

She is mild and clever. She obeys adults well. Her voice is loud. She looks cute and lovely. She is favored much by foster family and has been growing well there. She seems to adjust well.

It is sincerely hoped that the child will be adopted soon into a suitable family, who will give much care and love for the child's sound and bright future.

Q7: WHAT IS YOUR OPINION OF KOREA?

There is a belief among Koreans who embrace Won Buddhism that our destinies are determined by forces we cannot understand. That decisions have been made about our lives long before we are born. Pre-written.

Before I was born, it was written.

Before I was born, there was the war.

Before I was born, there was one mother and one father.

And I was born, as it was written.

And the rupture, too, was written.

I am writing into the rupture, the absence left there.

DAY 12: VISIT TO MT. SORAK (ONE OF KOREA'S MOST BEAUTIFUL MOUNTAINS)

In the last days of the trip, they take us to Mount Sorak. We stay in a resort hotel, play casino games.

It is as if we are the only people there. We wander the carpeted hallways with our paper cups filled with tokens. We drink cheap soju and laugh loudly. Spread ourselves across the pink couches in the lounge.

There is a late-night disco in the hotel and so we dance.

There is a private room for karaoke, and we sing American songs until we can no longer stand.

In those small hours, we talk about what we remember. What we think we can. Fleeting images.

A bowl of persimmons.

Dogs barking in a fenced yard.

A man in a dark suit, standing at a gate.

Or maybe we have dreamed them.

The way a dream can be a memory.

The way a memory can be a wish.

What must we call each other if we meet there

Brother sister neighbor   lover go unsaid what we are

Tens of thousands of names

Go unsaid the family name

— Myung Mi Kim,
from *Under Flag*

Q14: WRITE A LETTER TO YOUR MOTHER. (A LONG LETTER)

It is difficult to know how to begin. I read tips online:

Keep it short. Be sincere. Do not be overly emotional.

Do not make demands.

Do not use the qualifier "birth" mother.

Try not to go overboard about how good (or how bad) your life was.

Write by hand. Sign the letter. Use "Your daughter" or "Your son."

There are many false starts.

Q14: WRITE A LETTER TO YOUR MOTHER. (A LONG LETTER)

Dear ——

Hello. My name is Kim Mi Jin and I think you are my mother.

I don't think she would not recognize this name, so I try again:

Hello. My name is Mary-Kim Arnold, which was given to me by the American parents who adopted me in 1974. I was given a Korean name, Kim Mi Jin, when I arrived at the Orphans' Home of Korea, so there's no reason you would recognize me—not my name at least. I am enclosing a photograph of myself as a child.

Perhaps I should be more direct. Get right to the point:

I have been waiting my whole life to meet you.

But I fear this might be too aggressive.

Days pass. Then weeks. I try writing to one mother, but the other keeps pushing her way in.

I am the one who raised you. I am your real mother, she insists. But then she disappears again.

I am tired. Confused. I no longer remember what I thought this would accomplish. Even if I find her, what then?

What then.

Q14: WRITE A LETTER TO YOUR MOTHER. (A LONG LETTER)

I want to remember you

There is so much I don't remember

I want to tell you about my life now. Its joys. I want you to think of me happy—

my life, now—how far

from where it began.

Want you to know that I was good—did well

in school, did what I was told. Was quiet

when I was told to be quiet. Knelt when I

was supposed to kneel. Was pleasing. Gave pleasure.

You have been gone for so long

As a child, I thought you might come back—

you were a distant notion, a distant place to which

I could no longer return

distant star—barely visible, could make out its blurred edges, its pin-
prick of light—

no matter how far I reached out my arm I could not touch it.

I want you to be at peace. I want to mourn you in the proper ways.
Call your name

three times just to hold it in my mouth.

Name I do not know. Name I have never spoken, will never speak—

And to you, second mother: I suppose

I am still looking for you, too—

how you too have faded—all these long years gone.

You were there. Every day. You were happy once. You were proud—

the awards, the dance recitals, the performances.

You said that people would ask you at the grocery store, "Is she yours?"
China doll. You

were so proud and so ready for a fight.

"Yes of course she is mine"—or sometimes you would say

"Is that really any of your goddamn business"—

You were fierce. No other child was as good as me. Once the mother of
another child

said, "Our daughters are about the same." She was talking

about grades, or some sort of certificate I received, and you said,

"No, I don't really think so"—

You once told me that you read in the newspaper that there was a woman
trying to find homes for Korean children. You said my father asked, "What
do Koreans look like?"

But how could that have been true when there was the war?

Maybe I misremember. Maybe I want there to be more of a story than there is.

Once I asked you whether you had wanted to go to college. You did but your father didn't think it was possible. Daughter of immigrants. No one encouraged you. At your school, they gave you a pamphlet for the Woods Secretarial School and then you went. You went to work for men who looked through you, past you. Did not see you. How invisible you were.

No one saw you. Not your father, not your husband. Not even me.

There is so much I never knew about you. So much I can no longer remember. I am starting to forget.

You are there, but I cannot reach you.

There in that last room. It was white. I remember the curtains you chose. They were blue.

I sat by your bed. I held your hand. It felt so light. I watched the breath leave your body. I heard the sounds your body made. At first I thought

you were trying to speak—

the air coming up, the difficulty.

Years later, I would hear the wind whine through the hallway of my New York apartment building and gasp when the phrase came to me unbidden—*death rattle.*

They came to take your body away.

I let them take you. What else could I do?

In the end there was so little left—

clothing hung in your closet, things left unworn. You were saving them for celebrations that never came

We filled six trash bags with your things and drove them to the thrift store. I wish

I had kept them all.

I think of you so far away. I wonder what your life is now—

I have only what I have been given in the books I have read, the movies I have seen, the stories I have been told—

war-torn, poor, and desperate—only good for pleasing a man

and barely good for that.

I can't picture you.

It's not that I think I would have been better off there, but maybe I could have been better off knowing you—

You were born, perhaps between 1940 and 1950. As a girl, I picture you like the children we met in the countryside—white shirt, blue skirt. In a circle of friends, laughing. You were a happy child. Something happened as you got older. That is how it goes with girls. Your father got sick. Or your mother. It was difficult for him to take care of her alone. It was hard for him to watch and so he drank. He was lonely. He didn't have much help. She couldn't ask for things, and he couldn't help her. Your mother got sick. You saw her weaken. It made you feel like you had to make something of your life—

That is where the picture fades.

You are always disappearing, mother—

Mother, you were young, you were beautiful. You met a man. Your life changed. This is how it happens.

I am trying to keep you alive, in my memory.

I am trying to keep you alive—

I am waiting alone in a dark room for you to come back. You are not coming back.

I picture a street along the river when you were young

in the distance, some commotion—

what did you see

something small and quiet

border you can no longer cross

courtyard home you can no longer have

torn between wanting and not wanting.

I lived two years there, and not a word comes back, not a phrase, not the image of a single face, not the smell of a broom-swept house—

I want this to be something it is not.

Holding fragments is not the same as making a broken thing whole—

None of it familiar but wanting it to be.

Dear ████████████

I think about you a lot ████████████
████████████████████████████████
████████████████████████████████
████████████████████████████████
████████████████████████████████
████████

But it is hard to start writing you after this ████
break of time.
████████████████████████████████
████████████████████████████████
████████████ I spent the winter researching ████
████████ because
████████ I knew that ████████████
████████████████████████████████
████████████████████████████████
████████████████████████████████
████████████████████████████████

████████████████████ I wanted to talk about
my life ████████
████████████████████████████████
████████████████████████████████
████████████████████████████████
████ to understand ████████████ what
████████████████████
I was ████ to ████████ you
████████████████████████████████
████████████████████████████████
████████████████████████████████
a girl in the ████ frame
It is hard ████
████ to fit ████

ACKNOWLEDGMENTS

My sincere thanks to Carla Harryman for selecting this book and to the editors at Essay Press for their patience and support—in particular, Andy Fitch and Aimee Harrison. To Travis Sharp and Maria Anderson.

Unending thanks to Jen Bervin.

Thanks to Mary Ruefle and Maggie Nelson, who encouraged various parts of this work at various times. Thanks to Jamaal May. Thanks to Paul Lisicky.

Thanks to Ed Park. To Matthew Salesses, Kevin Fanning, Jimin Han, Alvin Park, Alexander Chee, and Janet Isserlis, whose early encouragement made everything possible. Thanks to Lori Freshwater, Adriana Cloud, and Jessica David. Thanks to Leigh Hendrix and Stephen Crocker.

Thanks to the editors and the journals who have published and promoted my work: Brooks Sterritt at *HTML Giant*, Kari Larsen and Ben Van Loon at *Anobium*, Masie Cochran at *Tin House (Open Bar)*, Molly Gaudry at *The Lit Pub*, Scott Garson at *Wigleaf*, Chris Moyer at *The Pinch Journal*, Lauren Spohrer at *Two Serious Ladies*, Liz Kay at *BurntDistrict*, Justin Daugherty at *Sundog Lit*, Courtney Dodson at *Day One*, Ian Sanquist at *Swarm*, Ruben Quesada and Rauan Klassnik at *Queen Mob's Teahouse*, Georgia Bellas at *The Atticus Review*, Chris Tonelli at *So and So Magazine*, Thibault Raoult at *Realpoetik* and *The Georgia Review*, Albert Mobilio at *Hyperallergic*. Thanks to Brian Blanchfield.

Thanks to Roxane Gay, Marisa Siegel, and *The Rumpus*.

Thanks to Don Mee Choi and Myung Mi Kim.

Thanks to the early teachers: Robert Coover, Carole Maso. Thanks to Mark Bernstein. Thanks to Eurydice Kamvisseli.

Thanks to Paula Krebs and Claire Buck.

Thanks to Darcie Dennigan, Tina Cane, Kate Schapira, and Kate Colby. Thanks to Elizabeth Schmuhl. Thanks to Donna Miele.

To Lauren Banks, Allison Grimaldi Donahue, Mo Duffy Cobb, Melissa Matthewson, Andrea Beltran, and Andrea Feldman.

To Norinda Arnold, Mira DaSilva, and Debra Larocchia.

To Matthew Derby, with more love, gratitude, and admiration than I can express.

This book is dedicated to my children, Zooey and William.

NOTES

PAGE XIII–XIV   I was introduced to the work of Theresa Hak Kyung Cha in 1997 by my graduate school advisor, Carole Maso. *Dictée* was the first significant work by a Korean American woman artist that I had encountered and the experience of reading it, struggling with it, emulating it, has had a profound and lasting influence on what I imagine possible in my own work.

For different reasons, I had been haunted by the short life and work of Francesca Woodman, first introduced to me by writer Max Winter, for some years when I realized that both she and Cha had both been in New York at the same time when they died. This is not in itself remarkable in a city of millions, but I began to imagine them, walking the streets of the city to which they each had only recently moved—Woodman from Providence in 1979, Cha from Berkeley in 1980—working, dreaming, their lives unfolding. I do not know that they ever met, but I hold in mind the image of a heat map of the city, with the spaces around each of them glowing red, pulsing.

Some common themes can be found in their work and they seem to have shared some influences—French surrealism, for example. Both women worked primarily in black and white and used their own bodies as subjects in their work.

Over the years, I have attempted several different projects to hold both these artists in mind, and to locate myself, as a woman artist, in conversation with them. This is one such attempt.

PAGE 1   This is from Cha's Personal Statement and Outline of Independent Postdoctoral Project, submitted to the Chancellor's Postdoctoral Fellowship, UC Berkeley in 1979, to continue work on the film, *White Dust from Mongolia.*

The statement comes from the Theresa Hak Kyung Cha Archive at the University of California, Berkeley Art Museum and Pacific Film Archive, and is referenced and contextualized in Ed Park's essay, "This is the writing you have been waiting for," which appears in *Theresa Hak Kyung Cha: Exilée; Temps Morts: Selected Works,* edited by Constance M. Lewallen.

PAGE 3   Excerpts from the "Social Study"—issued by Social Welfare Society of Seoul, Korea, dated September 5, 1973—appear throughout.

PAGE 7   The Korean television show "I Miss that Person," is a weekly 60-minute show to reunite separated families, which has aired on public broadcast station KBS since 1996. The show's website reports that as of 2007, 1,100 of the 2,094 people who have appeared on the show have been reunited with their lost families.

Over time, the network has developed services specifically targeted to overseas adoptees, including a video call-in capability, so adoptees living abroad can tell their personal stories live on television. Adoptees apply to appear on the show. The questionnaire is the first step in the application process.

PAGE 9   The "Education Program for Overseas Korean Adoptees," was hosted by the National Institute for International Education Development (NIIED) and the Ministry of Education, from June 28—July 14, 2000. All tuition and lodging expenses were provided by NIIED. We covered the costs of our travel.

PAGE 33   This line is from Rukeyser's 2006 poem "Käthe Kollwitz," about the German Expressionist artist.

PAGE 37   *The Memoirs of Lady Hyegyong* is considered to be one of the first significant pre-modern texts written by a woman in East Asia. Unlike other writings of the time which were composed in formal Chinese, Lady Hyegyong's memoirs were written in the common Korean script, Hangul.

PAGE 41   The sketch of the "Big House" is from Hildi Kang's *Family Lineage Records as a Resource for Korean History: A Case Study of Thirty-Nine Generations of the Sinch'on Kang Family (720-A.D.—1955)*, in which the author documents decades of research into traditional Korean lineage records called chok'po, through the generations of the Kang family into which she married.

When I first encountered this image, I had an immediate and unexpected visceral response to the simple elegance of the courtyard— the protection of its inhabitants that it suggested. Kang Sang-Wook, (Generation 38 of the Kang family) says of his drawing:

> Our Big House boasted a tile roof and rose above the ground on
> a platform of hewn stone. . . . A stone wall surrounded the com-
> pound of the Big House, and in the wall, a strong two-door gate

stood open during the day to welcome visitors. Inside the gate a courtyard spread out, with an earthen floor packed so hard that even when it rained the dirt didn't turn to mud. All around the four sides of the courtyard stood the rooms of the house, some detached and some built right into the wall.

This house, this land, had been in our family for five hundred years. We didn't think about it, we just accepted it—and expected it to continue another five hundred years.

PAGE 43   This from Donald Knox's introduction to his 1985 volume, *The Korean War: An Oral History, Pusan to Chosin*, in which he documents interviews with U.S. veterans of the Korean War. The paragraph in which the excerpted quote appears reads as follows:

In 1950 the Americans who arrived in the hundreds of thousands found Korea to be a country of high, rough-hewn mountains, steep, narrow valleys; wide, deep rivers; endless hills; threadlike paths; bad roads; heavy rain and deep snow; rice paddies and mud-plastered villages. And it smelled foul. Korea lacked charm or natural beauty and was neither quaint nor rustic. It should have been the last place on earth where anyone would want to fight a war.

I had to read and re-read those last sentences several times. The proposed logic that wars should be fought (that we should want to fight them) in places that are beautiful, charming, quaint or rustic is so baffling and enraging, it renders me nearly speechless.

PAGE 51   Cha's killer, Joey Sanza, worked as a security at the Puck Building in lower Manhattan. She was on her way there to meet her husband, photographer Richard Barnes, who was taking photographs the building's renovations. It took three trials to convict Sanza of her Cha's murder.

From the case record of the 1986 appeal of Sanza's conviction, this detail haunts:

> The police were initially unable to ascertain where Mrs. Cha had been murdered. However, her husband and her brother searched the building where defendant worked and found a room the police evidently had overlooked. Inside they found the victim's other boot, gloves, hat and button.

PAGE 89　In an interview with Bill Moyers in 1995, Adrienne Rich says:

> I think in this poem, what I am talking about is the choice that we can make, to move deeper into things, or simply to live worthily, maintain your attitudes, hold your position, even die bravely, but not to see what might have been seen. Not to grasp what might have been grasped. And that is a choice, for us all, whether in poetry or in life.

PAGE 113　This is my erasure of a letter Francesca Woodman wrote to Suzanne Santoro, dated June 18, 1980. The letter appeared in the exhibition publication, *Francesca Woodman Roma 1977-1981*, edited by Giuseppe Casetti and Francesco Stocchi, published on the occasion of the exhibition *Francesca Woodman photographs 1977-1981*, il museo del louvre, Rome, May 23-June 19, 2011.

BIBLIOGRAPHY

Barthes, Roland. *Camera Lucida: Reflections on Photography*. New York: Hill and Wang, 1981. Print.

Behrens, Melissa, and Jaimie Hauch. "Does Motor Development Influence Language Development." Marquette University, n.d. Web. 20 May 2015.

Cha, Theresa Hak Kyung. *Dictée*. Berkeley, CA. Third Woman Press. 1995. Print.

Cha, Theresa Hak Kyung, and Constance Lewallen. *Exilée; Temps Morts: Selected Works*. Berkeley: U of California, 2009. Print.

Fish, Stanley. *How To Write a Sentence and How To Read One*. New York, NY. HarperCollins. 2001. Print.

Fishman, Joshua. "What Do You Lose When You Lose Your Language." *Stabilizing Indigenous Languages*, n.d. Web. 20 May 2015.

Gumport, Elizabeth, "The Long Exposure of Francesca Woodman, *The New York Review of Books*, NYRblog, January 24, 2011.

Hyegyonggung, Hong Ssi. *The Memoirs of Lady Hyegyong*. Berkeley, CA: University of California Press, 1996. From the Introduction by JaHyun Kim Haboush.

Kang, Hyun Yi, Norma Alarcòn, and Elaine H. Kim. *Writing Self, Writing Nation: A Collection of Essays on Dictée by Theresa Hak Kyung Cha*. Berkeley: Third Woman, 1994. Print.

Kim, Myung Mi. *Under Flag*. Berkeley, CA: Kelsey Street Press, 1998. Print.

Knox, Donald. *The Korean War: Pusan to Chosin, An Oral History*. New York, NY: Harcourt Brace & Company, 1985. Print.

Lewallen, Constance, Lawrence Rinder, and T. Minh-Ha Trinh. *The Dream of the Audience: Theresa Hak Kyung Cha (1951-1982)*. Berkeley: U of California Berkeley Art Museum, 2001. Print.

Nelson, Stacy L. "International Adoption and Language Development." *Research Papers*. Paper 227. Southern Illinois University Carbondale. Web. 2012. 19 May 2015.

Phelan, Peggy, "Francesca Woodman's Photography: Death and the Image One More Time," *Signs*, Volume 27, No. 4, (Summer, 2002), pp. 979-1004.

Reines, Ariana, "An Hourglass Figure: On Photographer Francesca Woodman," *Los Angeles Review of Books,* April 4, 2013.

Sontag, Susan. *Susan Sontag on Photography*. London, Great Britain: Allen Lane, 1978. Print.

Steinhauser, Jillian, "Finding Francesca Woodman," *The Paris Review* blog, May 23, 2012.

Thang, Nguyen Tat. "Language and Embodiment." *VNU Journal of Science, Foreign Languages* 25 (2009): 250-56. Web. 20 May 2015.

Wallach, Amei, "Theresa Cha: In Death, Lost and Found," *New York Times*, April 20, 2003.

Woodman, Francesca, Ann Gabhart, Rosalind E. Krauss, and Abigail Solomon-Godeau. *Francesca Woodman, Photographic Work: Exhibition*. Wellesley, MA: Wellesley College Museum, 1986. Print.

Woodman, Francesca, Corey Keller, Jennifer Blessing, and Julia Bryan-Wilson. *Francesca Woodman*. San Francisco, CA: San Francisco Museum of Modern Art, 2011. Print.

Woodman, Francesca, Giuseppe Casetti, and Francesco Stocchi. *Francesca Woodman: Roma 1977-1981*. Vienna, Austria: AGMA, 2011. Print.

MARY-KIM ARNOLD is a poet and visual artist. Her work has been featured in a number of literary and art journals, including *Tin House*, *The Georgia Review*, *Hyperallergic*, and *The Rumpus*, where she was Essays Editor from 2013–2015. She was born in Seoul, and was raised in New York. She holds graduate degrees from Brown University and Vermont College of Fine Arts. She lives in Rhode Island.

이 우편물에는 아무것도 넣지 못하며 첨부하지도 못합니다
Nothing may be contained in or attached to this letter.